Fredegund, France

A Book of Poetry

RICHARD ROBINSON

Sunny Lou Publishing Company
Portland, Oregon, USA
http://www.sunnyloupublishing.com

2nd Edition: April 15, 2024
Original Publication Date: May 28, 2022

ISBN: 978-1-955392-67-9

Contents

Preface

Anyone who knows me well, and they come few and far between, knows that I'm a huge Francophile. It's in my blood or DNA, so to speak sillily. (Because I don't believe I have a drop of French blood in me!) But it is *that* deep, the phenomenon, the dream, the infatuation with France that has been haunting me for so many years, for decades.

I have said as much to various people, both French and non-French persons, over the course of the years, with mixed reactions. What sort of reaction was I expecting? I don't know, honestly. Probably a sympathetic one, something sympathetic souls might echo, those who have an appreciation of the "problem." For it is a problem, like just about everything in life. But the reactions I have received range anywhere from a bemused look, to a shared sentiment (at least verbally, but who can tell a person's soul?), to confusion, and finally even to a looking askance or away, as if in derision, short of rolling one's eyes. This latter reaction happened to me recently, in France of all places. Ah, well. What can I say, France is to me like a woman, the one that got away maybe, or a vintage bottle of wine that one drank once and could never find again. She is to me what Woman is, was, to Villiers.

> *The central preoccupation, the umbili-*
> *cus, of the singular poet that was the*
> *author of* The Future Eve *was, – and*

this is something that must be completely intolerable to imbeciles, – his really unprecedented need for a restitution of woman. So rare a manner of being that it is almost impossible to speak about it without seeming to solicit a padded cell for oneself.

I wonder if you read that carefully. I have just written these words: Restitution of Woman.

It has nothing to do with a pleading, with a dithyrambic paranymph, with such and such fawning praise for the dangerous Sex. It has to do with a renewal of earthly Paradise, after the harsh winter of six thousand years. It has to do with rediscovering that famous Garden of Voluptuousness, the symbol and accomplishment *of Woman, which all men gropingly search for throughout the centuries.*

– The Resurrection of Villiers de l'Isle-Adam, Léon Bloy.

I don't expect this book of poetry, *Fredegund, France*, to be read by many people, no more than ten or twelve probably, and as for those who do read it, I don't expect it to be understood. I don't flatter myself that its message is so very deep, or deep at all; it is, most assuredly, just the opposite: very banal. But it is personal and dear to *me*. And that has got to be good enough. Let imbeciles read it, misunderstand it, and disparage it if they want to. To which I can only respond, as "fresshe" May does in the Merchant's Tale, "I rekke noght".

I had a chance to visit France again recently, for the Nth time in my life, but this time rather uniquely for it was just after the recent apocalypse, which had descended on our world several years ago, had started to crawl back into the hole it had come out of, at least for now, by which I mean the viral pandemic of recent date, which has wrecked such havoc on all our lives, physically, materially, financially, morally, emotionally, psychologically, politically even.

For the one or two readers who might find this book and read it and share similar ideas of beauty as myself (assuming it contains any), enjoy!

– Richard Robinson, 2022 May 28

Fredegund, France

You who were my Belle, my Dear,
Although the source of my sufferance,
Are you not then always my Country,
So young and foolish like France?

– "Birds in the Night," *Romances sans paroles,* PAUL
VERLAINE

PART ONE

"And I'm going to France!"

The Feast

Months later I look out my window and see / Two
silhouettes of two leafless trees, hands raised to stop... – "A
Crack in the Sky; On a Path, a Winter Flower", *Ourigan,*
Oregon, WILLIAM CLARK, et al.

That is the dawn, blue and black,
Light blue and dark black, a backdrop of azure
Against which the angular branches of trees
Without leaves stand up. I recall

It being said "Stop." How many centuries ago?
When ink clouds passed, north
Or northeast, on their way to a feast
That we were not invited to.

            – Oregon, 2021

La Bonne Maman

And in this jar of purple jam,
All of France, all of it!
With its stickiness and hubris –
La Bonne Maman.

And I can do no better now, –
In the blueness of the hour, –
While it grabs at me like a *grisette*
Tripping on methamphetamines...

Memories of better years
When as a young man, without
Two nickels to rub together,
I boarded a plane and voilà:

It's Paris, the City of Lights,
The Pentapolis of pleasures,
La Moulin Rouge, let's go!
And Veronique the silent. Near

The Barbès–Rochechouart station,
In a bar near Montmartre,
Beneath the *Basilique du Sacré Cœur*,
– I have my memories! –

As a young man, young I say,
And a bartender's wife, not pretty,
Round a small table, holding a
Hypothetical bottle of champagne, –

Who is angry, and who brandishes a knife?
It's the bartender's wife's husband,
A good man from Antony,
Not taking no for an answer.

And at that school, and in those days,
That's how we learnt our French,
Not like today where I'm reading the
Label of a jar of jam, far away.

And I'm Going to France!

"You're stubborn!" – "And I'm taking you / To the country."... – Poem XVII, *Odes In Her Honor,* PAUL VERLAINE

I'm on this plane with two good friends, –
What are their names again? – ah, yes:
Edgar Allan Poe and Paul-Marie Verlaine,
And only the elegant stewardess might guess
What the three of us have in common.

Eddy and Virginia, holding hands,
Sit in a row by themselves, for their love
Is a venture between his wife and a man,
And it suits them amorously like a glove,
For she is young and he handsome.

Poor Lelian slouches, a *crayon* in hand,
Affecting to look out the porthole, a Pernod
In the other, while his cousin,
Or wife, eludes him in his other thoughts
More poignantly than in the *jardin*.[1]

And me, I sit alone, but my little blind
Is shut, like my future, and I dream on Mei
Whom, yet another child wife, I found
The nearest thing on earth to joy.
No tears, heart: this plane will land soon.

---

[1] *jardin: Ayant poussé la porte étroite qui chancelle,/Je me suis promené dans le petit jardin...,* from "Après Trois Ans," *Poèmes Saturniens,* Paul Verlaine.

Galswinth in the Grove of Cypresses

...And I loved her. – Septentrion, JEAN RASPAIL

*... the salience of her haughty temples, the subtle oval of
her cheeks, the cruel upturned nostrils that trembled in the
wind of peril, ... the chin of a taciturn despoileratrix, that
always serious smile... all that in its entirety,... grew into
the most magnificent seduction...* – Akédysséril, VILLIERS DE
L'ISLE-ADAM

The beauty of your lines, the roundness of your belly,
Soft, glaucous girl like a prepubescent cone,
Brown later, brown-gray like a discard, like a detritus,
The cone of a gymnosperm, let's call you a cypress.

I love to whisper things in your ears,
Tickle the tendrils at a level with my feet, and
Tease out the word-seeds from your strobilus.

My doe, my dear, my very female deer,
Gift of God from on high, west of Byzantium,
You may call me Cyparissus II, but...

You know and I know I am an acorn,
A son of an oak. And you should wash your face... –
Your face! Your face, the face of France,
Your face is like a battle ax to me,
With a socketed head, gleaming like metal,
Whispering at me, brushing my strings,
Like etesian breezes on scaly branches,

Cleaving my virtue and my maturity,
Calling to me, your haft, to cut you down.
And I will cut you down, on an estival day,
And I will call you Brigid.
And you will lie down with me in the forest
Weary of the hunt and major hallali.
And my javelin, my javelin will invade you.

As for what comes next, let's call it a clade –
What matter if the sowing be barren.
And my grief will be your grief, and
Our griefs will be so much wider than the horizon.

Christ in the Garden of Olives

Dans une rue, au cœur d'une ville de rêve, / Ce sera comme quand on a déjà vécu... – Kaleidoscope, PAUL VERLAINE

And I will shiver on that pew, beside the limestone
       columns,
And the wood will be hard and the columns cold,
And my shoulder will lean into yours, o Léon Bloy,
And our *Aves* and *Paters* will echo throughout the
       nave.

And I will grow weary on that bench finally, with
       merely my paraclete,
And my prayers will fall flat on the floor like
       damaged angels,
And other visitors will slap them, step on them,
       make them bleed,
And I will know then that it is time for me to leave...

But the Christ in Gethsemane will catch my eye
And I will be drawn to its blues and black, its reds
       and gray
And the day will start to grow long again, and my
       time infinite,
On the butte of Montmartre, in the Church of Saint-
       Peter.

Clodovech and Clotilde

Chlodovech and Clotilde, in the misty grey
Of a late afternoon, along the banks of Yssel.
And I'm at a bar in old town Lille,
By the train station, or I think I am,
      And wishing I were in Tournai.

    Alone, always alone. Drink, eat, breathe...

In Metz now, at the cathedral of St. Stephen,
Yellow in the tooth, like the complexion of your skin.
And Brunhildis you are not, and I am not Chilperic,
But I might wish to be, – do you wish me to be?
      I will be him if you will be her...

    Alone, always alone. Drink, eat, breathe...

Silva Carbonaria

Confitebor tibi in cithara, Deus, Deus meus. Quare tristis es, anima mea? et quare conturbas me? – PSALMS, 42:4-5

And here I am at the edge of a wood,
Behind me a plain and pasturage.
This Færie wood like a river that,
Of great spannage, must be breached.

O Queene of the wood, grant me the courage
For I aspire, but wither before you,
To enter into this dark, cold foliage
From a pasturage so sunny and blue.

Silva Carbonaria 2

*A civilized man in a civilized society will want nothing more
than to be uncivilized: the mark and measure of his
civilization is the strength of his desire to flee it. –*
ANONYMOUS

At the edge of a wood, a solitary wood,
At the edge of a solitary wood where I live
And breathe – in my dreams.

No birds there but nightingales and budgies,
Sparrows and finches, but no pigeons or crows
In the wood where I live – in my dreams.

That wood is a curtain, that curtain is made of trees:
White oak, silver birch, poplar, European beech.

There is a wood in my head that is a partition
Made of beech: it is the land I come from
And the land where I aspire to be.

# # #

And the wood is a forest.
And there is no end to this forest.
Silver-grey bark, yellow leaves, gray in winter.
And the absence of *one* leaf in the foliage today,
Like a hole in the sky, leaves an emptiness in my
            mind,
Where the slate-gray azure fills it, insufficiently.

The drab-pale leaves of this forest,
Whereon a day, one early morning, a sun so pale
Rose one finger's breadth north of Fredegund,
Standing there, naked like a leaf.

These beech trunks like bars of a prison. –
I wanted you to love me physically, emotionally,
And I wanted you to treat me like your possession,
And me you, and you me, and you, and me...
My paramour, my fief, your prerogative, your
        demesne.

And the trees, I see them now, are yellow and grey
        and silver,
And I am no more knowing of them,
Standing near them, with them before my eyes,
Than if I were in another hemisphere.

And I give them the names of my former wives:
Fredegund, Brunhilda, Basina of Thuringia...

And the sun, a white circle, beams behind a fog;
It is a finger's width south of where it was yesterday.
And I know no more of the sun today than I do of
The ceiling above the trees in the woods beneath the
        vault
Where I wander – in my dreams.

Black Leafs

...multis Francorum apud Carbonariam ferro perimptis. –
GREGORY OF TOURS

Black leafs in a black winter,
In the Silva Carbonaria;
And if they're not black, they're grey;
And if they're not grey, they're yellow.
But with Ætius coming, there's no place to hide.
And a mild autumn *in memoria*.

Ætius my crupper!
Smells more like barren sticks
And beech leaves in decomposition.
The fresh smell of his fetid insolence:
I know my master when I see him,
And Ætius he is not.

PART TWO

Ah, France, France!

Une Boulangerie[2] gourmande

And if I say *bonjour*, and if I give a smile,
In a singsong manner, in a voice with some grace,
Like a bird on a wire, near the place Paul Verlaine,
In the vicinity of Butte-aux-Cailles,

Where the Moulin-des-Prés[3] looks down,
Once upon a time, on the Bièvre,[4]
An underground reach of water, dirty-brown,
On a certain day, at a certain hour,

And if the patroness of La Lorette,
A "Boulangerie gourmande," who is anything but,
Unhesitatingly responds, *bourgeoisement,*
Bonjour! singsongingly, – have I then arrived?

– Paris, 13th arrondissement, 2022 May 9

---

[2]*boulangerie*: a bakery and (sometimes) pastry shop.

[3]*Moulin-des-Prés*: literally the "wind mill of the meadows," near the Butte-aux-Cailles, or "hillock with quail."

[4]*Bièvre*: a river that flows through (or rather *under,* today) Paris and is tributary to the Seine.

Pont des Trous[5] de Tournai

Toutes mes langueurs rêvassent – "Bruxelle, simples
fresques," – *Romances sans paroles,* PAUL VERLAINE

Over this river Scheldt that the French call Escaut,
The Germans *schol*, and the English *shoal*, float
All my languors, all my dreams,
All my youthful memories it seems

Of a life lived, or not lived, bad or well;
A breeze blows softly on my cheek, and well
Do I know, strongly do I feel, that there is no space
To turn around on this bridge and embrace.

We must wait; but time walks through
And water flows under this *Pont des trous*,
That spans our lives, this old Gothic bridge
With holes in it, spanning the Escaut.

And no matter how much I might want to turn back,
To turn around, to retrace my tracks,
The train station that I disembarked from
Grows infinitely distant, and it is dark.

And no matter how much I might want to turn
          around,
To turn back in time, to go over lost ground,

---

[5]*Pont des Trous*: from French, "Bridge with Holes."

The church bells keep pealing, and I'm lost,
I'm lost in the streets of this town.

– Tournai, 2022 May 11

L'Hôtel Moderne de Metz

And the pigeons' cooing from beneath the rooves,
Immeasurable guttural sounds rolling in soft waves,
Echoed from the whitewashed walls of a large inner
        courtyard
Crowned by terracotta scallops, red with black molds.

And a matutinal sunlight, pale vanilla, in the stucco
        folds
Within the space of an empty Cistercian courtyard,
Filled my rented room, resplendent in soft waves
Of trembling light devoid of human sentiment
        beneath the rooves.

    – *Metz, 2022 May 13*

The Fondness

Avril est mort d'amour et nos âmes sont vieilles — Les roses mortes, foulées... – "Ronde," *Joys,* FRANCIS VIELÉ-GRIFFIN

The empty wooden chair you did not sit in,
In that small Italian restaurant, by St. Etienne's
            Cathedral;
The salad, the plate of pasta *aux aubergines*
You did not eat. The conversation we did not hold,

The glass of sparkling water you did not drink.
The memories we did not share, like revenants
Hankering after a past once lived together; the plans
We did not make, one warm evening in Metz.

The hand I did not take, stepping over cobblestones,
Walking aimlessly through streets. The words
You did not whisper in my ear, under the moon's soft
            light,
Pale against the night, paler than your shoulder.

The misunderstanding not clarified, the silences kept,
The fondness we failed to foster or reciprocate.

– Metz, 2022 May 14

In the Place St. Louis

Que rêviez-vous l'été dernier / Parmi les moissons jauni-
ssantes? / Un rêve qu'il faut renier / Et qui s'effeuille au
creux des sentes, " – "Mai Fleuri", *Joies*, FRANCIS VIELÉ-
GRIFFIN[6]

"Le paysage dans le cadre des portières / Court
furieusement, et des plaines entières... " – Poem VII, *La*
Bonne Chanson, PAUL VERLAINE

The scene in the frame under the arches
Arrests all my appetencies in Mays and Marches,
When I find myself distant from the loved one,
South of Eifel, east of Ardennes,

In the stark air of an Austrasian blue sky,
With no bees, no cicadas, and no lilies to arraign,
To stop it, to stop my languorous heart,
      To stop it from languishing;

No, love, not a single cloud was in that azure sky,
Immaculate like your face, on that naiadian day,
And the argentine tintinnabulation of your voice...

But the ancient casuistry of cascading rooves,
Stepping stones that lead me away from you,
      Away from your heart,
Hard like Jaumont stone, dirty-yellow golden,

---

[6]Que rêviez-vous...: French for "What were you dreaming last
summer/Amidst the yellow harvests?/– a dream I must
renounce/And that drops its leaves into the hollow of footpaths,"
"Blown May," *Joys*, Francis Vielé-Griffin.

So special to Metz, from *Montois-la-Montagne*
      In Lorraine...

Originally from the Orne, tributary to the Moselle,
Whose two rivers' waters lazily float you,
Float you away from me, away from my desire...

And the pink, Ophelian parasols that hide my intent
Under a hundred skies, their tables fully set,
      but without guests, –
They are exasperating to the cafe owner
And waitress almost exploding with impatience.

    – Metz, 2022 May 15

... Between Notre-Dame de Dijon & the Next Menu Prix Fixe

Seated in the *place des Ducs de Bourgogne,*
In a very small garden that the *Guide Michelin* forgot,
Beneath neo-gothic windows of the palace wherein John
The Fearless and his father Philip the Bold rot,

With its open-air walkways, well-kept grasses,
And gurgling fountains, – on benches, wooden and modern,
Old men talk, younger men gawk, and local lasses
Presumably without a *sou* in their pockets ask for alms

Under the still paternal regard of Philip the Good,
Under the *tour de Bar*, built to keep his enemies,
And espy them from afar, while goodman Jaquemart
And Jaqueline his wife strike, 5 minutes early, the bell.

As for me, I'm outside the *Gîte Bons Ami*s, my hotel,
Trying to identify where I lost my will on
The road between Moses in the *Chartreuse de Champmol*
And *la Chouette,* that tourists run their fingers along...

-- Old Town Dijon, 2022 May 18

La Fontaine Jeunesse

... Soudain, tournant vers moi son regard émouvant: /
"Quel fut ton plus beau jour?" fit sa voix d'or vivant...
– *"Nevermore", Poèmes Saturniens,* PAUL VERLAINE

"Dear one," my wife said to me, "in all Dijon,
What, what was your fondest memory?" I looked at
            my son.
And I recalled the sumptuous funereal sarcophagi
Of *Jean Sans Peur* and his father *Phillipe le Hardi*

In the Museum of Fine Arts, the *Palais des Ducs de*
            Bourgogne;
And I recalled the bronze Jacquemart and Jacqueline
With their two children, ringing the bells, before the
            hour;
And I recalled Gothic churches, medieval buildings...

"My fondest memory, dear one," I said, "was
            'Youth'."
A humble water fountain in Darcy Square, near St.
            William's Gate:
Three children sitting atop a rock, naked,
Looking at three frogs looking back at them agape.

            – *Place Darcy, Dijon, 2022 May 19*

Apricots in Avignon

I have eaten the plums that were in the icebox
– "This is just to say," WILLIAM CARLOS WILLIAMS

Wepyng and waylyng, care and oother sorwe / I know
ynogh, on even and a-morwe. – "The Merchant's
Prologue," *The Canterbury Tales,* GEOFFREY CHAUCER

Abricots in Avignon, *moutard* in Dijon,
And in Nancy, ah Nancy: the *muguet*.
Do not ask me why, I cannot say.

And yet, at a certain hour, on a certain day,
I was thinking of leaving Avignon
Having only just arrived in that place.

A heavy languorousness hung in the air, –
An overcast sky, sure sign of the *Borasco* –
Made me overly solicitous, anxious for my care.

Thief of love, executioner without pity,
You encircled my heart, o you *lou Sudestou*,
Exacting tears, cries, cares and other misery.

Countless years of listlessness, on a day,
From out the blue, out the Mediterranean,
Rained down on me, with a fierce *furia*.

You overwhelmed my heart, –
Avignon, oh Avignon! of France,
On the banks of the Rhône, in Occitania.

– Avignon, 2022 May 21

The Passion

For HENRY DE GROUX.

Except for the woman floating tranquilly almost on
        her back,
In a sea of angry people, a throng seemingly, an
        attack –
Her face pallid, eyes wide open, looking to heaven,
"What have we done, Lord?" is the facial expression
Or "Why can't you save yourself?" – Flowers float
In her hair, which flows golden-brown, honey-golden
Like a field of wheat in France, or Belgium,
Onto a presumptive ground, and into the bruised grin
Of a man holding out a soft hat with dark waxy brim,
Green like poblano peppers, red inside, phallic even
Post-coitus, limp like a weary, weathered Anthurium.
Another woman in a similar pose, in yellow tunic,
Just behind the first, eyes wide, head tossed back,
Looking to heaven, asking – "Why Lord, why?!"
A child cries, wails. Several do.
One of the women must be his dying mother.
A white dog, rabid, with studded collar, face
Of a skull even, if one squints, or a rabid hound
        chasing
After a woman's leg, to bite it, hidden beneath a rich,
        blue mantle.
A sprig in her out-held hand, it is Brunhilde's
        "handle,"
And the expression on her face is calmness,
        incantative.

Is she a witch? No one can say. Next to her are
        ghouls,
Mouths open, howling; a bearded man, like Moses;
Horses, demons, teeming, swarming, towards the
        outraged Christ   ,
who takes it all in stride, wears a rich red mantle
Falling from his shoulders, and a loin cloth looking
More like Renaissance breeches. People are drawn to
        him like satellites
To a black hole, in a forsaken heaven, iron filings to a
        magnet.
And a Roman soldier with thick biceps threatens the
        crown
With a long iron rod, seems to stab a man in the arm.
Behind him a naked torso, of another man, bound, the
        Good Thief maybe.
A wooden cross and ladder complete the scene; white
        clouds
Like seagulls, or wraiths, squawk in an angry sky.

        – *Palais du Roure, Avignon. 2022 May 21*

PART THREE

There is no France in France anymore.

The Bise Bites

The Bise bites, as if a myriad of bees
Were stinging the knuckles, the cheeks.
Having thrown off his blankets like sleep,
Winfrith stood, tent flaps flapping,
On the outer verge of the Silva Carbonaria.
"I know this place." he said.
His eyes stoked the embers of a new day,
Another eye, bloodshot, peeped up over the horizon.

Throwing off sleep like a blanket,
Winfrith emerges, behind him the flaps of the tent,
Stokes with his eyes the embers of a new day
The fiery lashes, on the horizon, of another eye.
No Brunhildis in his tent, this day, cold,
       complaining...

The Bise bites, it is as if a myriad of bees
Were stinging the knuckles, the cheeks.
Throwing off sleep like a blanket,
Winfrith emerges, behind him the flaps of the tent,
Stokes with his eyes the embers of a new day
The fiery lashes, on the horizon, of another eye.
No Brunhildis in his tent, cold, disdaining...

You Scorned Me

It did not matter that you scorned me.
You abused me with your slanting smile.
The sun at morning filled the horizon
With all the redness of your pudenda.

Did it matter that you scorned me?
Did I have to ask myself, years away,
Why you did it, why you abused me
With your slatternly smile, virgin?

Galsuenda

Sed per amorem Fredegundis... – GREGORY OF TOURS

And you, Fredegund, you will have me dead,
Unless I manage to free myself first.
Dark-haired Fredegund, pale-skinned Fredegund,
Like ancient alder buds in cold February.

And like Fredegund, you will have me dead
Unless I manage to free myself first,
Galswinth, daughter of Athanagild...

And like St. Hilarion, I am tormented in my cave.
And I might want you as I could have you, free,
And you could have me as you once wanted me,

Radegund, Fredegund, Brunhild,
Basina of Thuringia, Ingund, Aregund,...
Clotilde, of the sun-golden blonde hair,
Bathild, with the dark eyelashes, stoking fires.

And the apples I tasted taste of the both of you.
And the alder buds I saw hinted at either childhood.
And as beads of sweat gathered on my lips
Like dew drops on early morning grapes,
In eastern Francia, with southern hints and
              reminiscences,
As I chopped wood to heat *la viande* in a morning sun

You sat in a padded chair and bathed in blown heat,
Sipped honeyed mead from a demi-tasse,

Auto-phantasmagorified robuster loves,
But farther from nature, behind panes of glass.

Riparian

Don't you see it? – there! in the mist,
That shimmering palace where the lilies blow;
Where Sylvie gets lost in the leaves, and... and...
Emile's Tamar loses it on the bitumen maybe;
Don't you see it?! I know I see it.

Don't you see it? there! in the light of the sun,
Where children run down to the river,
And men lounge on floats espying women,
Along the Rhine and Moselle, along rivers,
When being a young man was fun sometimes...

You see it then, don't you? I see it.
Frogs in the mud, Childeric and the bees,
Pinot Gris, baguettes, cheese,
The Cathedral of Saint Stephen, first martyr,...
You see it, don't you see it? I see it.

Thinking on Marianne

We are not young anymore, but we can try...
But you wanted a purse to go with your beauty mark,
And I wanted a postcard bride, someone to fall in
        love with,
Or try; for me a pale muguet, for you a business
        suit.

For you see, there is no poetry in *such* retribution:
I do not see France in your pants now. And when you
        smile,
You smile darts and lances, and my heart shrivels
On boughs; and there is no America in your glances.[7]

The revolution and revolution of golden wheat fields
While, as a young thigh, you pumped powerful pedals
And made the world gyrate; – but where are you now,
        blonde Rose, April blue bells;
And the fields you passed, are they now fallow?

I ramble in the wind, leaning sadly over iron railings,
Thinking on Marianne, undone for all my failings.

---

[7]no America in your glances: *je n'ai jamais rêvé d'autre amérique*,
"Dea," *Cull of April*, Francis Vielé-Griffin.

Mr. Vincent Vander Gogh

All the girls in silver wigs and deep
Dank voices, come and go
Babbling on about Mr. Vincent Vander Gogh.

Let's run away then, me and you,
Pure vestiges of a forgotten race,
From all the madness in our saintly lives,
When the fog is stretched out against the lower Rhine
        like... fog.
For there is nothing *here*, and
Life is always on the horizon, on the other side
Of the bush, river, mountain, bridge, silva,... –
Like an inexorable question: shall we live?
If live, where live, and when?
Today, July twenty-nine, or August thirty-first...
Did we ever live? Do we know what it means to live:
To live, – I want to live! And yet...
The only answers I seem to acquire,
The only yields I harvest,
Are false *fleurs de lis* in stagnant water.

All the girls, with picts on their skin and metal
In their mouths, come and go
Babbling on about Mr. Vincent Vander Gogh.

After the Fancy

After the fancy, – Neustria, Austrasia.
My heart continued to belong to Audovera,
Audovera the good, Audovera the chaste,
While my pants, my pants belong to Fredegunda,
Fredegunda the domesticated, *une tarte aux abricots*,
Not much more than that.

> While sap ran in the veins,
> While the bloom of youth was on,
> While sugar seethed in the cane,
> While the hem of her skirt
> Skirted her foot.

The girls of France today – but who looks at them?
They are all Radagunda, isn't that right?
Or Radagunda or Galswintha, maybe.
While my pants, my pants belong to Fredegunda,
Fredegunda the maid, *une tarte aux framboises*,
Not much more than that.

> While sap runs in the veins,
> While the bloom of youth is on,
> While sugar seethes in the cane,
> While the hem of her skirt, –
> The hem of her skirt...

Laus Perennis

Aujourd'hui, l'Action et le Rêve ont brisé
Le pacte primitif par les siècles usé...
– "Prologue," *Poèmes Saturniens*, VERLAINE

And gone are the days of *gestes*, and tonnes
Of cider, or ambrosia, or fermented mead
Quaffed between daybreak and three, and the need
For damsels in forgotten towers to get undone,
The Veleda, and the hordes of blonde *leudes*,
Lying in "wait" in the Septentrion. And I,
Like a Sigismund, foreseeing myself dead
At the bottom of a well, and hearing
Above the aqueous and glaucous swell
The stagnant echoes of a *laus perennis* –
Not for me, not for me, not for me...

Other Books by the Publisher

Fanchette's Pretty Little Foot by Restif de La Bretonne

Je M'Accuse... by Léon Bloy

My Hospitals & My Prisons by Paul Verlaine

Salvation Through the Jews by Léon Bloy

Words of a Demolitions Contractor by Léon Bloy

Cellulely by Paul Verlaine

Ecclesiastical Laurels by Jacques Rochette de la Morlière

Flowers of Bitumen by Émile Goudeau

Songs for Her & Odes in Her Honor by Paul Verlaine

On Huysmans' Tomb by Léon Bloy

Ten Years a Bohemian by Émile Goudeau

The Soul of Napoleon by Léon Bloy

Blood of the Poor by Léon Bloy

Joan of Arc and Germany by Léon Bloy